go figure

Use your mathematical skills to explore computer games, solving puzzles and completing missions along the way to become a master gamer!

LEARN ABOUT IT
RATIOS

⟩GO FIGURE!

4:3

5:4

16:9

16:10

This section will take you through the mathematical ideas you'll need to complete each mission.

The practical examples in this section will test your knowledge of the ideas you've just learnt.

ANSWERS AND GLOSSARY

Answers to the Go Figure! challenges can be found on page 28. Words in *italics* appear in the glossary on page 30.

You might find some of the questions in this book are too hard to do without the help of a calculator. Ask your teacher about when and how to use a calculator.

WHAT EQUIPMENT DO YOU NEED?

Pen or pencil

Notepad

Protractor

SCREEN READY

First things first – you need to get your screen set up properly. This means choosing the correct *aspect ratio* and the maximum number of pixels.

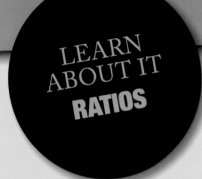

LEARN ABOUT IT
RATIOS

Ratios compare two or more things, such as two lengths.

In this instance, we use a ratio to describe the relationship between the length and the height of a computer or TV screen. For instance, a TV screen that has 1280 pixels across and 1024 pixels up has a ratio of 1280:1024.

To work out the *simplest form* of a ratio, you need to keep dividing each number by the same number until you get the smallest whole number possible, as shown below. So the ratio 1200:900 ($\div$30) = 40:30 ($\div$10) = 4:3, which is its simplest form.

The same simple ratio can be used to describe several different numbers. So a screen with 1280 pixels across and 800 pixels up is in the same ratio as one measuring 1680 x 1050 pixels = 16:10.

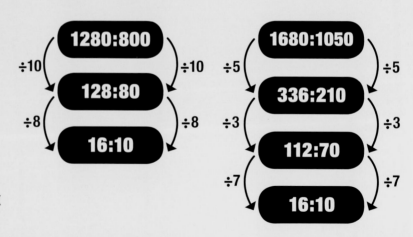

1280:800
$\div$10 $\div$10
128:80
$\div$8 $\div$8
16:10

1680:1050
$\div$5 $\div$5
336:210
$\div$3 $\div$3
112:70
$\div$7 $\div$7
16:10

[A Maths]

JOURNEY

<=~±÷ ›through‹

Computer

Games

CONTENTS

04 SCREEN READY

06 HIGH-SPEED DRIVER

08 MONEY MAZE

10 LEADERBOARD SCORES

12 3D CHALLENGE

14 WAR WIZARDS

16 JET FIGHTER

18 ISOLATION

20 AIM AND FIRE

22 ACCURACY RATINGS

24 TRANSFORMING TROOPS

26 SHAPE SHOOTER

28 GO FIGURE! ANSWERS

30 MATHS GLOSSARY

32 INDEX

It is easier to compare ratios when in the form n:1, where 'n' might be a *decimal*. To get this, divide both numbers in the ratio by the second number.

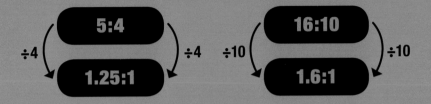

÷4 (5:4 / 1.25:1) ÷4   ÷10 (16:10 / 1.6:1) ÷10

〉GO FIGURE!

The higher the number of pixels your screen has, the better the resolution and the clearer the pictures will be. Use your knowledge of ratios to work out the answers to the questions below.

05

Common aspect ratios for displays

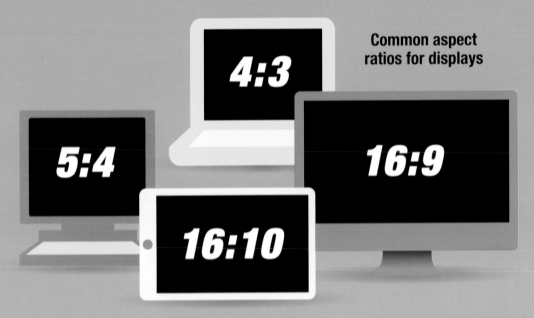

5:4

4:3

16:9

16:10

....

1 An old screen has 640 x 480 pixels.
a) Which of the above aspect ratios is it?
b) Does it have the same aspect ratio as a 1024 x 768 screen?

2 You look at a screen with 1920 pixels across and 1200 pixels up.
a) Which of the aspect ratios is it?
b) Write this as a ratio in its simplest form.

3 Many gamers believe that the best ratio for gaming is 16:9. What is this ratio in the form n:1? Use a calculator to help you find n to two decimal places. (Find out more about rounding on page 15.)

4 An ultra-high-definition screen has 3840 x 2160 pixels. Would this be suitable if you wanted to get a screen with the aspect ratio 16:9?

HIGH-SPEED DRIVER

It's time to burn some rubber with this super-speedy driving game. You need to monitor your lap-times and speeds to see if you can end up on the leaderboard.

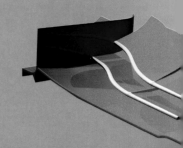

LEARN ABOUT IT

SPEED, DISTANCE AND TIME

The time, t, a car takes to travel a particular distance, d, at an average speed, s, can be shown by the formula:

$$t = d \div s \quad \text{or} \quad t = \frac{d}{s}$$

So the time, in hours, it would take a car to go a distance of 6 miles, travelling at an average speed of 120 miles per hour (mph) can be found like this:

$$t = 6 \div 120 = 0.05 \text{ hours}$$

Multiply by 60 to find the number of minutes:

$$0.05 \times 60 = 3 \text{ minutes}$$

Multiply this number by 60 to find the number of seconds:

$$3 \times 60 = 180 \text{ seconds}$$

For a car travelling 9 miles at 160 mph:

$$t = 9 \div 160 = 0.05625 \text{ hours}$$

$\times 60$

$$= 3.375 \text{ minutes}$$

$\times 60$

$$= 202.5 \text{ seconds}$$

〉GO FIGURE!

Here are the fast-lap players' boards for two different tracks:

FAST-LAP PLAYERS' BOARD					
TRACK 7 – DISTANCE 8 MILES			TRACK 8 – DISTANCE 15 MILES		
NAME	TIME (IN SECONDS)	POSITION	NAME	TIME (IN SECONDS)	POSITION
JED	179.5	1	AMY	342.5	1
KIM	182.5	2	JOE	358.5	2
AMY	185	3	JED	386.5	3

1 Here are some of your times for tracks 1 to 5, given in minutes. Write each of these times in seconds: a) 1 minute b) 1.6 minutes c) 4 minutes d) 2.5 minutes e) 2.8 minutes.

2 When driving track 6, which has a distance of 9 miles, you have an average speed of 135 mph. How long does it take you: a) in minutes? b) in seconds?

3 You record a fast time on track 7, at an average speed of 160 miles per hour. a) How many seconds did it take you? b) Into which position would this get you on the fast-lap players' board?

4 You have several attempts at track 8. Your average speed each time is 135 mph, 160 mph and 180 mph. How many of these laps appear on the players' board and in which positions do they appear?

MONEY MAZE

Use the *coordinates* to guide yourself around the maze and collect some big-money prizes.

08

A coordinate grid can have four *quadrants*, with the centre being the origin where the x- and y-axes cross.

You can refer to any point by giving its co-ordinates. The coordinates are two numbers in brackets. The first shows the distance you have to go across on the x-axis. The second shows the distance you have to go up or down on the y-axis.

The point (x, y) on the grid to the right is at (3, 4) because, from the origin, you go 3 squares to the right and 4 squares up to reach the point.

All points on the right of the y-axis have *positive* x *values.* All points on the left of the y-axis have *negative* x values. All points above the x-axis have positive y values. All points below the x-axis have negative y values. So the point (a, b) is at (-3, -4).

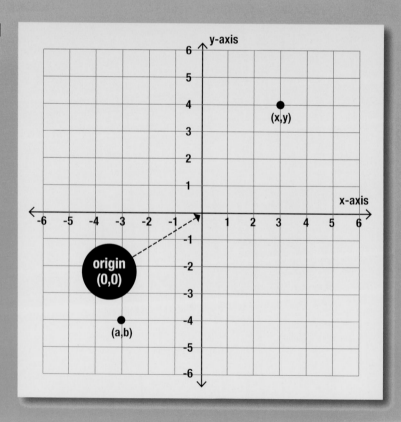

❭GO FIGURE!

Here is your money maze. Find the route that will win you the most money.

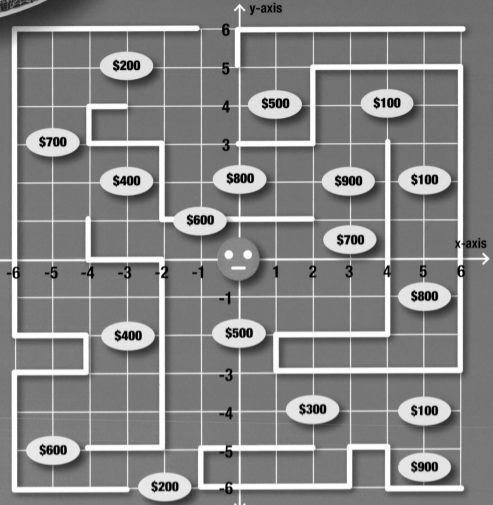

09

1 Start at the origin each time and visit the points, moving in a straight line each time. Pick up the money as you pass it! How much will you win?

Route 1: (0, 0) → (0, -4) → (5, -4) → (5, -6)

Route 2: (0, 0) → (3, 0) → (3, 4) → (5, 4) → (5, -2)

Route 3: (0, 0) → (3, 0) → (3, 2) → (0, 2) → (-3, 5) → (-5, 5) → (-5, -1) → (-3, -1) → (-3, -3) → (-5, -5)

2 **What is your total money for the three routes?**

LEADERBOARD
SCORES

In this game, you must collect points as you travel around a virtual city in a police helicopter. For each item you collect you score points. For each crash or collision you lose points.

LEARN ABOUT IT
LARGE NUMBERS AND PLACE VALUE

When using large numbers, it is important to know the value of the digits and to line them up from the right when adding or subtracting.

When adding 10,040 (ten thousand and forty) to 1,426,709 (one million, four hundred and twenty-six thousand, seven hundred and nine) we can just add 1 to the ten-thousands (TTh) digit and 4 to the tens digit:

Billions			Millions			Thousands			Ones		
HB	TB	B	HM	TM	M	HTh	TTh	Th	H	T	U
					1	4	2	6	7	0	9
				+			1	0	0	4	0
				=	1	4	3	6	7	4	9

It is so easy, you can actually do the adding in your head! Just make sure you know which digits to change.

Subtracting can be done in the same way. Here is 24,586,794 − 1,002,090

Billions			Millions			Thousands			Ones		
HB	TB	B	HM	TM	M	HTh	TTh	Th	H	T	U
				2	4	5	8	6	7	9	4
			−		1	0	0	2	0	9	0
			=	2	3	5	8	4	7	0	4

〉GO FIGURE!

You're flying the helicopter through a city following a dangerous suspect on the ground. These are the scores for your flight:

STARTING SCORE
1,220,694 POINTS

AVOIDED MISSILE
SCORE 15,000 POINTS

COLLIDED WITH BIRD
LOSE 5,100 POINTS

HIT BY GUNFIRE
LOSE 120,000 POINTS

NARROWLY MISSED SKYSCRAPER
SCORE 20,400 POINTS

WENT UNDER A BRIDGE WITHOUT CRASHING
SCORE 500,000 POINTS

1. What is your final score?

2. **How much more than your starting score was your final score?**

3. Will your flight get you onto this leaderboard, and if so, in what position?

RANK	NAME	SCORE
1ST	CLY	1,680,000
2ND	ZTR	1,635,000
3RD	JAY	1,630,999
4TH	DIN	1,630,993
5TH	SAM	1,630,256

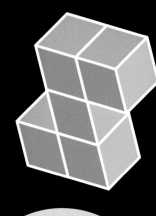

3D CHALLENGE

For this game you need to select and match three-dimensional (3D) shapes made from cubes. Each time you succeed you score points according to the *volume* of each shape.

LEARN ABOUT IT
3D SHAPES AND VOLUME

3D shapes have three dimensions – length, width and height.

The amount of space that a 3D shape takes up is called its volume, and is measured in cubes – usually centimetre cubes (cm^3) or metre cubes (m^3).

The shape on the left has been drawn on *isometric paper* to show it is 3D. If each small cube is 1 cm^3 then the volume of the whole shape is 10 cm^3, assuming that the two blue cubes are on top of two other cubes.

When viewed from different angles, a 3D shape can look very different. Sometimes some of the cubes are hidden from view. Here is a shape with a volume of 5 cm^3, viewed from different angles:

We can also twist the shape to see it from other angles, like this:

12

⟩GO FIGURE!

In this game you must remove one cube from each of the shapes shown to create pairs of identical shapes.

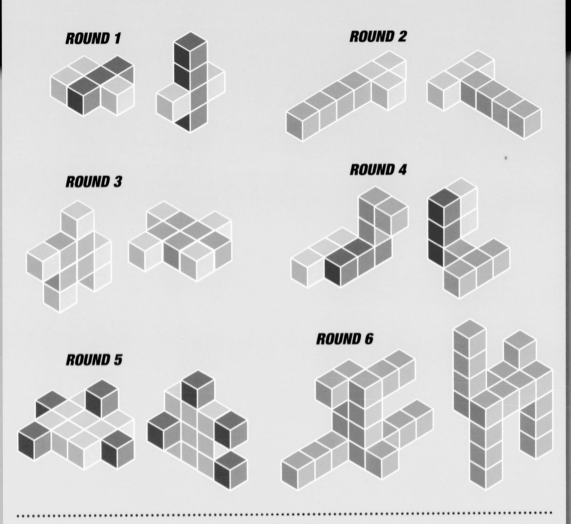

ROUND 1

ROUND 2

ROUND 3

ROUND 4

ROUND 5

ROUND 6

1 Taking each round at a time, choose a cube from each shape to remove to leave two identical shapes.

2 Remembering that each small cube has a volume of 1 cm³, find the volume of the final identical shape for each round.

3 You score 1000 points for each 1 cm³ of volume. What do you score for each round?

4 What is your total score for rounds 1 to 6 all together?

WAR WIZARDS

You must buy wizards in the *War of Wizards* game. Each wizard is given a box with 100 pieces of stone, which they try to turn into diamonds. Can your wizards make more diamonds than your enemy's?

LEARN ABOUT IT
PERCENTAGES AND VALUE FOR MONEY

Percentages (%) are fractions with the denominator 100, so 75% = $^{75}/_{100}$

If someone is expected to get something right 75 times out of 100, we can say that they have a reliability percentage of 75 per cent. This can be shown as a diagram, like the one on the right.

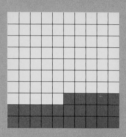

14

When comparing items to see which is the best value for money, find out how much you get for each unit of money, such as for each £1 or per token. Do this by dividing the amount by the total price.

To compare these bags of gems, divide the weight by the price.

1.24 kg

1.24 kg costs £10
$1.24 \div 10$
= 0.124 kg
per £

1 kg

1 kg costs £8
$1 \div 8$
= 0.125 kg
per £

0.6 kg

0.6 kg costs £5
$0.6 \div 5$
= 0.120 kg
per £

So for each pound you get more gems with the 1 kg pack.

To find out which wizard in the game has the best reliability percentage, you need to divide their percentage by their cost. For instance:

90%

90% for 50 tokens
$90 \div 50$
= 1.8% per token

54%

54% for 36 tokens
$54 \div 36$
= 1.5% per token

30%

30% for 18 tokens
$30 \div 18$
= 1.67% per token

So the best value is the first wizard since 1.8 is greater than 1.5 and 1.67.

If a calculator shows a number with many digits after the decimal point, round the number to two decimal places. Look at the third digit after two decimal places. If it's 5 or more, the second digit goes up 1. If it's 4 or less the second digit stays the same.

1.933333333 can be written as **1.93** (to 2 decimal places)

1.627906977 can be written as **1.63** (to 2 decimal places)

⟩GO FIGURE!

This table shows the reliability percentage rating and price for each wizard. Each wizard has a box of 100 pieces of stone. You and your enemy have 80 tokens each to buy wizards. You can both buy the same wizard.

WIZARD	RELIABILITY % RATING	PRICE
Warlock	84%	48 tokens
Astra	70%	43 tokens
Shem	60%	34 tokens
Oberon	58%	30 tokens
Japheth	50%	27 tokens
Kasper	48%	25 tokens
Zorn	40%	21 tokens
Filton	33%	18 tokens
Theo	28%	16 tokens

1 If given 100 pieces of stone to turn to diamonds, how many diamonds would you expect to get from: a) Warlock? b) Astra? c) Japheth? d) Filton?

2 For each wizard in the table: a) Find the percentage value per token that you would get (to 3 decimal places). b) Find the wizard who gives you the best value per token. c) Find the wizard who gives you the worst value per token.

3 It costs the same to buy Shem as it does to buy Filton and Theo together. Would you expect to get more diamonds from Shem or from Filton and Theo?

4 Your enemy chooses to buy Astra, Zorn and Theo with his 80 tokens. How many diamonds would he expect to get altogether?

5 You now must choose how to spend your 80 tokens. You do not have to use them all. a) Which combination of wizards is likely to get you the most diamonds for your money? b) How many diamonds would you expect to get?

JET FIGHTER

Your next quest involves flying a supersonic jet as fast and as accurately as possible. Each phase of the game has increasingly difficult challenges.

LEARN ABOUT IT
TIME INTERVALS

Times can be shown using colons and decimal points, like this:

3:40 means 3 minutes 40 seconds
3:40.99 means 3 minutes 40 seconds and 99 hundredths of a second.

3:40.99

minutes   seconds   hundredths of seconds

When adding times it is important to remember that 100 hundredths of a second becomes an extra second, 60 seconds becomes an extra minute, and 60 minutes becomes an extra hour.

3:59.97 3:59.98 3:59.99 4:00.00 4:00.01

On this timer, one hundredth of a second is added each time.

When adding **4:56.40** and **0:00.61**, notice that we will get 101 hundredths of a second, so the number of seconds in the answer is increased by one, to give **4:57.01**.

4:56.40 + 0:00.61
= 4:57.01

When adding **4:57.01** and **0:03.00**, notice that we will get 60.01 seconds, so the number of minutes in the answer is increased by one to give **5:00.01**.

`4:57.01` + `0:03.00`

= `5:00.01`

When adding **55:59.50** and **0:00.50**, notice that we will get 100 hundredths of a second and therefore we then get 60 seconds, so the number of minutes in the answer is increased by one to give **56:00.00**.

`55:59.50` + `0:00.50`

= `56:00.00`

⟩GO FIGURE!

Here are your fastest times for each phase of your jet fighter experience.

PHASE	TIME
▶ TRAINING	10:20.00
▶ PROFICIENCY	05:05.50
▶ AEROBATIC MISSION	01:03.50
▶ ADVANCED TRAINING	10:01.03
▶ WINGED COMBAT	02:30.50
▶ MAJOR COMBAT MISSION	03:56.87
▶ ULTIMATE CHALLENGE	09:45.78

1 In the training phase, how many seconds was your time under 11 minutes?

2 In the ultimate challenge, how many hundredths of a second was your time under 9 minutes 46 seconds?

3 a) Find the total time taken for the first two phases. b) Now add the third time to find the total time for the first three phases. c) Continue to add each time in this way, and find your total time.

4 How much less than 43 minutes is your total time?

MISSION 8

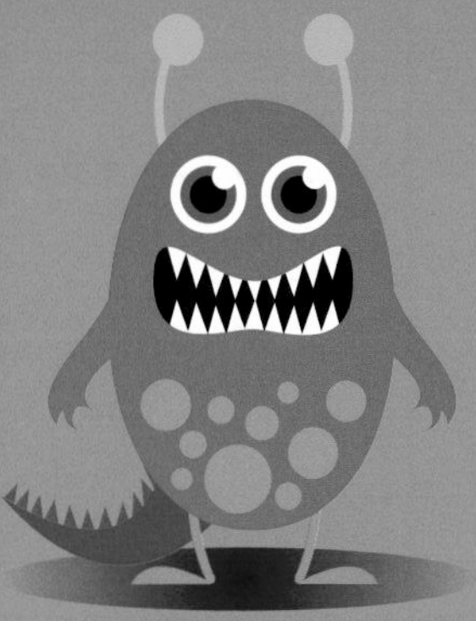

ISOLATION

For this game you must isolate the monster, leaving him in a room alone without a number. The two rooms are linked and there are special rules about how to remove things from the room that you must follow, or the monster will eat you!

LEARN ABOUT IT SOLVING EQUATIONS

What is in one room must be equal to what is in another room: if a number is put in one room, the same number must also go into the other room. If a number is taken out of one room, it must also leave the other room.

Here we can remove the **+7** from the left-hand room by doing the inverse, the opposite, by subtracting 7.

But if we do it to one room we must do it to the other.

This leaves us with the monster on its own in the left hand room and 15 – 7 = 8 in the right hand room.

To isolate the monster, the number in the other room must be **8**!

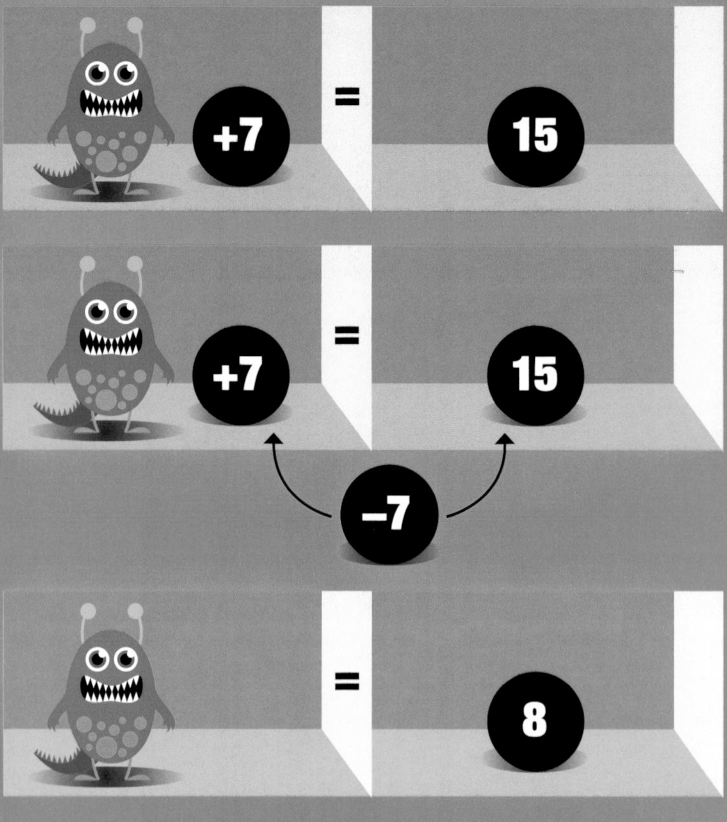

Use the inverse for each *operation*, like these shown here:

 +7 inverse **−7**   **×10** inverse **÷10**

−9 inverse **+9**   **÷5** inverse **×5**

Remember, if you remove a monster from one room, you must remove one from the other room too!

❯GO FIGURE!

Use the inverse operation method to remove the number from the room with the monster in and isolate it.

puzzle 1   **puzzle 2**

puzzle 3   **puzzle 4**

puzzle 5

1. Find out what one monster is equal to for each of these puzzles, using the rules of the game.

2. **Make up a similar monster puzzle where the monster is equal to:**
   a) 6 b) 10 c) 100

3. Make up a puzzle that has three monsters in one room and two in the other, where each monster is equal to 3.

AIM AND FIRE

For your next game you must learn how to fire a missile and how to avoid incoming enemy missiles.

LEARN ABOUT IT
LINEAR GRAPHS

Linear graphs are straight lines shown on a coordinate grid. The coordinates of each point along the straight line share something in common.

Remember, coordinates are always given as the point along the x-axis followed by the point along the y-axis:

20

Look at this line. Here are some coordinates of points along it:
(-5, -4) (-2, -1) (-1, 0) (1, 2) (3, 4) (5, 6)
Can you see any patterns?

Notice that the y coordinate is always equal to the x coordinate plus 1.

We can describe this line using the equation:
y = x + 1

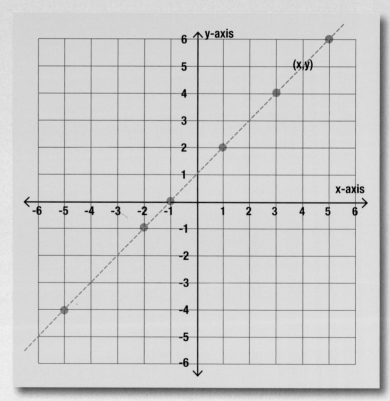

We can also predict whether other coordinates are along this line or not. For example, **(6, 3)** is not on this line as the y coordinate is not one more than the x coordinate.

For this mission you must accurately fire missiles
from your fighter jet and avoid the enemy gunfire.

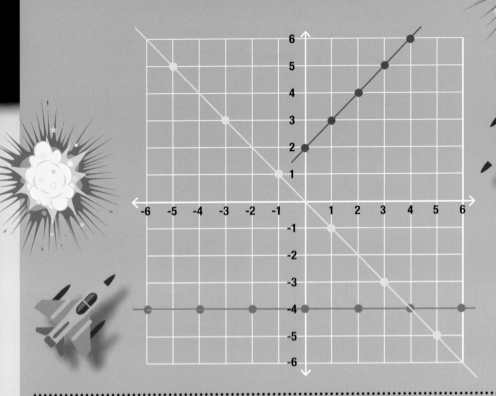

1 You need to program your missile to
pass through the following targets,
marked in red on the grid above:
(0, 2) (1, 3) (2, 4) (3, 5) (4, 6)
a) Look at the coordinates and write
down the pattern of the x and y
coordinates. b) What equation would
you use to program the missile?

2 a) Write the coordinates of the
targets marked in green on the grid
above. b) What do you notice about
the y coordinate of each of the
points along the green line?
c) What equation would you use
to program this missile?

3 a) Write the coordinates of the targets
marked in yellow on the grid above.
b) What do you notice about the x and y
coordinates of each of the points along
the yellow line?
c) Which of these equations would
result in the yellow path?
y = x   y = 2x   y = 5   y = -x

4 A missile has been programmed
using the equation y = x − 3.
Complete the coordinates to show
points along the missile's path:
a) (5, ??) b) (3, ??)
c) (-2, ??) d) (-3, ??)

5 If you are at (2, -1), do you need to
take action to avoid the missile from
Question 4 striking you?

ACCURACY RATINGS

The game *Dinopotomas* tests your skills in moving around a world of dangerous creatures. Scores are calculated as percentages that give an accuracy rating.

LEARN ABOUT IT
FRACTIONS AND PERCENTAGES

Parts of a whole can be expressed as fractions by putting the part on top of the fraction and the whole on the bottom.

For example, if you scored 200 points out of a total 800 points, this can be written as the fraction $\frac{200}{800}$.

Fractions can then be written in their simplest form by dividing both numbers by their largest *common factor* to give a smaller fraction. Here, both numbers can be divided by 200 to give the fraction ¼. Sometimes it is easier to divide several times to reach the simplest form.

$$\frac{200}{800} \overset{\div 200}{\underset{\div 200}{=}} \frac{1}{4}$$

$$\frac{77}{140} \overset{\div 7}{\underset{\div 7}{=}} \frac{11}{20}$$

$$\frac{3060}{7650} \overset{\div 10}{\underset{\div 10}{=}} \frac{306}{765} \overset{\div 3}{\underset{\div 3}{=}} \frac{102}{255} \overset{\div 51}{\underset{\div 51}{=}} \frac{2}{5}$$

Fractions can also be expressed as percentages, which are easier to compare. To write a fraction as a percentage, where the denominator (the bottom number) is a factor of 100, find what you must multiply it by to get 100. Then multiply both numbers by that number. The percentage is the top number of the answer. Here are some examples:

$$\overset{\times 25}{\underset{\times 25}{\frac{1}{4}}} = \frac{25}{100} = 25\%$$

$$\overset{\times 5}{\underset{\times 5}{\frac{11}{20}}} = \frac{55}{100} = 55\%$$

$$\overset{\times 20}{\underset{\times 20}{\frac{2}{5}}} = \frac{40}{100} = 40\%$$

⟩GO FIGURE!

These accuracy ratings have been calculated by finding the proportion of mistakes made out of the total number of tasks.

NAME	NUMBER OF MISTAKES	TOTAL NUMBER OF TASKS	FRACTION	FRACTION IN SIMPLEST FORM	%	ACCURACY RATING (100% - PERCENTAGE)
JHK	200	800	$\frac{200}{800}$	$\frac{1}{4}$	25%	75%
SID	8	40				
PET	50	200				
DAN	9	100				
JUL	34	200				
ZAK	21	75				

1. Copy out the table and complete it by calculating the accuracy ratings for:
   a) SID b) PET c) DAN d) JUL e) ZAK

2. **Which two players have the same accuracy rating?**

3. a) Who has the highest accuracy rating?
   b) Who has the lowest accuracy rating?

4. **Write the players in order, starting with the player with the highest accuracy rating.**

5. If you only made 6 mistakes out of a total of 150, how much better would your accuracy rating be than the best of the other players? Give your answer as the number of percentage points.

TRANSFORMING TROOPS

In the game *Ancient Civilisation*, you are responsible for ordering where the troops should go. You must give accurate directions to your troops to ensure that your civilisation is not destroyed.

LEARN ABOUT IT
GEOMETRICAL TRANSLATIONS AND PYTHAGORAS' THEOREM

24

In maths, a translation is when a shape or object is moved in a particular direction without rotating or reflecting it. You can translate horizontally, vertically or diagonally.

When describing a diagonal translation we say how many units across and how many up or down the movement is. Here you can see a *right-angled triangle* created by the horizontal, the vertical and the diagonal lines of this diagonal translation.

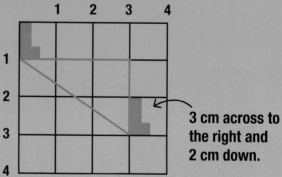

3 cm across to the right and 2 cm down.

Pythagoras' theorem gives us information about the relationship between the sides of right-angled triangles. It states that the sum of the *square numbers* of the two shorter sides of the triangle is equal to the square of longest side. This is shown by the formula:

$$a^2 + b^2 = c^2$$

where **a** and **b** are the shorter sides and **c** is the diagonal (sometimes called the hypotenuse).

We can use the formula to find the length of the diagonal line, using the horizontal and vertical lengths, like this:

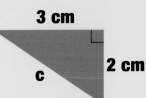

3 cm

2 cm

c

$3^2 + 2^2 = c^2$ $9 + 4 = c^2$ $13 = c^2$

We use the square root $\sqrt{\ }$ to find the value of **c**. $\sqrt{13} = c$ so **c = 3.6 cm** (to one decimal place).

〉GO FIGURE!

You want your troops to go to different cities on this map. Remember that 1 cm represents 1 km.

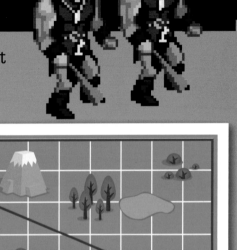

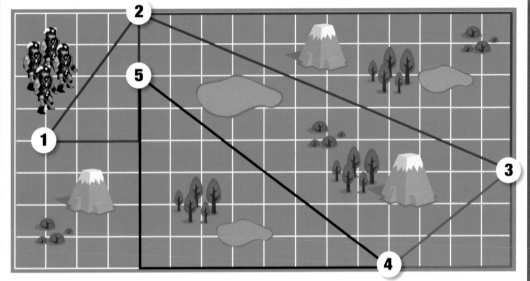

1. You must first order your troops to move from 1 to 2. Use the green triangle to help you describe the translation to move your troops. Give the number of kilometres to the right followed by the number of kilometres up.

2. Use Pythagoras' theorem to work out the length of the diagonal line from 1 to 2 to tell your troops how far to march.

3. Give the order for moving from 2 to 3, describing the translation in terms of horizontal and vertical distances. Use Pythagoras' theorem to work out the diagonal distance that the troops must march.

4. Now repeat for the marches from a) 3 to 4 and b) 4 to 5.

5. What is the total marching distance for your troops if they march from 1 to 5 via the diagonal lines shown?

SHAPE SHOOTER

For your final mission you must take a spaceship into the stratosphere to destroy fragments of a space station that recently exploded. This mission is vital to save the world!

LEARN ABOUT IT
ANGLES AND QUADRILATERALS

Angles are measured in degrees, with 90 degrees (90°) in a right angle (a quarter-turn) and 360° in a full turn.

An *angle* less than 90° is called an *acute angle*. Angles between 90° and 180° are called *obtuse angles*. We use a *protractor* to measure and draw angles, lining up the centre of the protractor with the corner of the angle, like this:

Be careful to count around from zero to the line. This angle is only 50° not 130°.

Anti-clockwise

Quadrilaterals are two-dimensional (2D) shapes with four straight sides. Here are definitions of special types of quadrilaterals:

Parallelogram: two sets of *parallel* lines **(a, b, c, d)**.
Rectangle: four right angles. It is a type of parallelogram **(a, d)**.
Square: four right angles and four sides of equal length; it is a type of rectangle **(d)**. **Rhombus:** two sets of parallel lines and four sides of equal length; it is a type of parallelogram **(c, d)**.

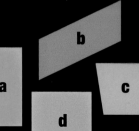

Trapezium: one set of parallel lines; one of the parallel lines is longer than the other **(e, f)**.
Kite: two short sides *adjacent* and of equal length, and two longer ones adjacent and of equal length **(g, h)**. If a shape with four straight sides doesn't match any of the descriptions we just call it a **quadrilateral (i)**.

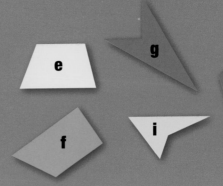

⟩GO FIGURE!

You must calculate the angles necessary to pinpoint your missiles so they hit and destroy the fragments before they fall to earth.

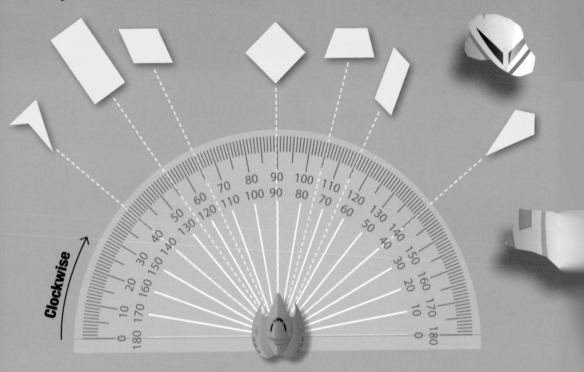

1 If you set a missile to be fired at 90° to the horizontal line of your spaceship, what shaped fragment of the exploded space station would you hit?

2 Reading the angles in a clockwise direction, is it true that firing at 115° would hit a parallelogram?

3 Through what clockwise angle should you set the missile to fire to hit:
a) the (non-square) rectangle?
b) the trapezium?

4 What shaped fragment would you hit if you fired at a clockwise angle of 140°?

GO FIGURE! ANSWERS

04–05 Screen ready

1. a) 640:480 = 4:3 b) 1024:768 = 4:3, so it does have the same ratio
2. a) 1920:1200 = 16:10 b) 16:10 = 8:5
3. 16 ÷ 9 = 1.78, so the ratio is 1.78:1
4. Yes

06–07 High-speed driver

1. a) 1 x 60 = 60 seconds
   b) 1.6 x 60 = 96 seconds
   c) 4 x 60 = 240 seconds
   d) 2.5 x 60 = 150 seconds
   e) 2.8 x 60 = 168 seconds
2. a) 9 ÷ 135 = 0.066 x 60 = 4 minutes
   b) 4 x 60 = 240 seconds
3. a) 8 ÷ 160 = 0.05 x 60 = 3 x 60 = 180 seconds b) Second
4. Two would appear: 300 seconds would be first, 337.5 seconds would be second

08–09 Money maze

1. Route 1: 500 + 300 + 100 + 900 = $1800

   Route 2: 700 + 900 + 100 + 100 + 800 = $2600

   Route 3: 700 + 900 + 800 + 200 + 700 + 400 + 600 = $4300
2. 1800 + 2600 + 4300 = $8700

10–11 Leader-board scores

1. 1,220,694 + 15,000 – 5100 – 120,000 + 20,400 + 500,000 = 1,630,994
2. 1,630,994 – 1,220,694 = 410,300
3. Yes, fourth

12–13 3D Challenge

1.

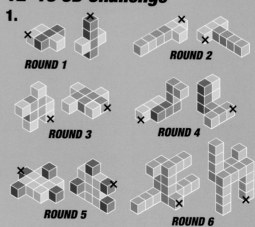

ROUND 1 ROUND 2 ROUND 3 ROUND 4 ROUND 5 ROUND 6

2. 5 cm^3, 6 cm^3, 8 cm^3, 8 cm^3, 12 cm^3, 17 cm^3
3. 5000, 6000, 8000, 8000, 12,000, 17,000
4. 5000 + 6000 + 8000 + 8000 + 12,000 + 17,000 = 56,000

14–15 War wizards

1. a) 84 b) 70 c) 50 d) 33
2. a) Warlock 84 ÷ 48 = 1.750
   Astra 70 ÷ 43 = 1.628
   Shem 60 ÷ 34 = 1.765
   Oberon 58 ÷ 30 = 1.933
   Japheth 50 ÷ 27 = 1.852
   Kasper 48 ÷ 25 = 1.920
   Zorn 40 ÷ 21 = 1.905
   Filton 33 ÷ 18 = 1.833
   Theo 28 ÷ 16 = 1.750
   b) Oberon c) Astra
3. Shem has a reliability percentage of 60, but Filton and Theo have a combined percentage of 61, so they would produce the most diamonds
4. 70 + 40 + 28 = 138 diamonds
5. a) Oberon, Kasper and Zorn will get you the most for a cost of 76 tokens (30 + 25 + 21) b) 146 (58 + 48 + 40)

16–17 Jet fighter

1. 40 seconds
2. 22 hundredths of a second
3. a) 10:20.00 + 05:05.50 = 15:25.50
   b) 15:25.50 + 01:03.50 = 16:29.00
   c) 16:29.00 + 10:01.03 + 02:30.50 + 03:56.87 + 09:45.78 = 42:43.18
4. 16.82 seconds

18-19 Isolation

1. Puzzle 1: 15 ÷ 3 = 5
   Puzzle 2: 13 + 6 = 19
   Puzzle 3: 4 x 4 = 16
   Puzzle 4: remove a monster from each to leave 9
   Puzzle 5: remove a monster from each, then 8 − 3 = 5
2. Answers will vary
3. Answers will vary

20–21 Aim and fire

1. a) The y coordinate is always 2 more than the x coordinate b) y = x + 2
2. a) (-6, -4) (-4, -4) (-2, -4) (0, -4) (2, -4) (4, -4) (6, -4) b) The y coordinate is always -4
   c) y = -4
3. a) (-5, 5) (-3, 3) (-1, 1) (1, -1) (3,-3) (5, -5)
   b) The x and y coordinates have the opposite sign: when x is positive, y is negative, and vice versa c) y = -x
4. a) (5, 2) b) (3, 0) c) (-2, -5) (-3, -6)
5. Yes

22–23 Accuracy ratings

1. a) SID: $^{8}/_{40}$ = $^{1}/_{5}$ = 20% 100 − 20 = 80%
   b) PET: $^{50}/_{200}$ = $^{1}/_{4}$ = 25%
   100 − 25 = 75%
   c) DAN: $^{9}/_{100}$ = 9%
   100 − 9 = 91%
   d) JUL: $^{34}/_{200}$ = $^{17}/_{100}$ = 17%
   100 − 17 = 83%
   e) ZAK: $^{21}/_{75}$ = $^{28}/_{100}$ = 28%
   100 − 28 = 72%
2. JHK and PET
3. a) DAN b) ZAK
4. DAN, JUL, SID, JHK and PET, ZAK
5. $^{6}/_{150}$ = $^{4}/_{100}$ = 4% 100 − 4 = 96%, so your accuracy would be 5 percentage points better than the best score

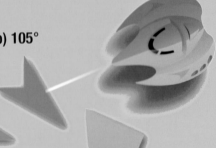

24–25 Transforming troops

1. 3 km to the right, 4 km up
2. $3^2 + 4^2$ = 9 + 16 = 25 √25 = 5 km
3. 12 km to the right and 5 km down
   $12^2 + 5^2$ = 144 + 25 = 169
   √169 = 13 km
4. a) 3 → 4: 4 km left and 3 km down
   $4^2 + 3^2$ = 16 + 9 = 25 √25 = 5 km
   b) 4 → 5: 8 km left and 6 km up
   $8^2 + 6^2$ = 64 + 36 = 100
   √100 = 10 km
5. 5 + 13 + 5 + 10 = 33 km

26–27 Shape shooter

1. Square
2. Yes
3. a) 55°, b) 105°
4. Kite

MATHS GLOSSARY

ACUTE ANGLE
An angle that is less than 90°.

ADJACENT
Two sides of a shape are adjacent if they share the same angle.

ANGLE
The amount of turn, measured in degrees.

ASPECT RATIO
The ratio between the width and height of a shape.

BILLION
A thousand million.

COMMON FACTOR
A number that can divide exactly into two or more other numbers.

COORDINATES
A series of numbers that will locate a point against axes.

DECIMAL
A number with a decimal point in it. The digit to the left of the decimal point is the number of units, while the digit to the right is the number of tenths.

DENOMINATOR
The bottom number in a fraction.

EQUATION
An equation is when two expressions are equal to each other, such as $3 + a = 8$. Equations can be solved by finding the value of the letter or letters, such as $a = 5$.

ISOMETRIC PAPER
Paper marked with equally spaced lines or dots to help you to draw pictures of 3D shapes and some 2D shapes.

LINEAR GRAPH
A graph in which points are connected by straight lines to show how something changes in value.

NEGATIVE NUMBERS
Numbers on the other side of zero from positive numbers. We write them using the minus sign (-), e.g. -5, -3, -7.

PERCENTAGE
A percentage is a special fraction which has a denominator of 100, e.g. $42\% = {}^{42}/_{100}$. Per cent means 'for every hundred'.

POSITIVE NUMBER
A number that is greater than zero.

PROTRACTOR
A mathematical instrument, shaped in a circle or a semi-circle. It is marked with degrees and used to measure angles.

PYTHAGORAS' THEOREM
The square of the long side of a right-angled triangle (the hypotenuse) is equal to the sum of the squares of the other two sides. This can be written as $a^2 + b^2 = c^2$, where a and b are the two shorter sides and c is the hypotenuse.

OBTUSE ANGLE
An angle that is between 90° and 180°.

OPERATION
A mathematical process carried out on one or more numbers to produce another number. The four most common operations are addition, subtraction, multiplication and division.

PARALLEL
Lines or shapes that never meet and are always the same distance apart.

QUADRANT
One of the four sections created when a shape is divided by two lines that cross, such as the x-axis and y-axis.

RATIO
Ratios show how one or more numbers or values are related to another. So a ratio of 2:1 shows that there are twice as many of the first value as there are of the second.

RIGHT-ANGLED TRIANGLE
A triangle that has a right angle, 90°, as one of its angles.

SIMPLIFY/SIMPLEST FORM
To simplify a fraction, we change it to an equivalent fraction that uses smaller numbers, e.g. $\frac{6}{8} = \frac{3}{4}$. When a number cannot be simplified, it is in its simplest form. Ratios can also be simplified in the same way, 4:12 = 1:3.

SQUARE NUMBER
The number we get by multiplying a number by itself, written using the symbol ^{2}. So 2^2 means 2×2, 3^2 means 3×3 and so on.

TRANSFORMATIONS
These are ways of changing or moving a shape. There are four main types of transformations: reflection, rotation, translation and enlargement.

VALUE
The total amount that a number or group of numbers adds up to.

VOLUME
The amount of space an object takes up. It is measured in cubic units, such as cubic centimetres (cm^3) or cubic metres (m^3).

INDEX

addition 10–11
angles 26–27
average 6–7

coordinates 8–9, 20–21
decimal 5
decimal points 15, 16
decimal places 15
denominator 14, 23
distance 6–7

equations 18–19
fractions 22–23
hypotenuse 24
inverse 18, 19
kite 27
linear graphs 20–21

negative values 8
operation 19

parallelogram 26, 27
percentages 14–15, 22–23
place value 10
positive values 8
protractor 26
Pythagoras' theorem 24–25

quadrants 6
quadrilaterals 26–27

ratios 4–5
rectangle 26, 27
rhombus 26
right-angled triangles 24–25

shapes 12–13
simplest form 4
speed 6–7
square (shape) 26
squares 24
square root 25
subtraction 10–11

time intervals 16–17
three-dimensional (3D) 12–13
translations 24–25
trapezium 27

value for money 12–13
volume 12–13

32

WEBSITES

www.mathisfun.com
A huge website packed full of explanations, examples, games, puzzles, activities, worksheets and teacher resources for all age levels.

www.bbc.co.uk/bitesize
The revision section of the BBC website, it contains tips and easy-to-follow instructions on all subjects, including maths, as well as games and activities.

www.mathplayground.com
An action-packed website with maths games, mathematical word problems, worksheets, puzzles and videos.

ACKNOWLEDGEMENTS

Published in paperback in Great Britain in 2018 by Wayland

Copyright © Hodder and Stoughton, 2016

All rights reserved

Editor: Elizabeth Brent

Produced by Tall Tree Ltd
Editors: Joe Fullman and Rob Colson
Designer: Ed Simkins

ISBN: 9780750298506

Wayland, an imprint of Hachette Children's Group
Part of Hodder and Stoughton
Carmelite House
50 Victoria Embankment
London EC4Y 0DZ

An Hachette UK Company
www.hachette.co.uk
www.hachettechildrens.co.uk

Printed and bound in China

10 9 8 7 6 5 4 3 2 1

MIX
Paper from responsible sources
FSC® C104740

The website addresses (URLs) included in this book were valid at the time of going to press. However, it is possible that contents or addresses may have changed since the publication of this book. No responsibility for any such changes can be accepted by either the author or the Publisher.

Picture credits
4tl iStockphoto.com/yelet, 4cl iStockphoto.com/colematt, 6-7 iStockphoto.com/Henrik5000, 8-9 iStockphoto.com/dem10, 10tl iStockphoto.com/fcknimages, 10-11 iStockphoto.com/guvendemir, 14tl Dreamstime.com/Chuckchee, 16-17 iStockphoto.com/ Robin Hoood, 18-19 iStockphoto.com/PinkPueblo, 20-21 iStockphoto.com/Zelimir Zarkovic, 22tl JoeLena, 22cl iStockphoto.com/CoreyFord, 22bl iStockphoto.com/Naz-3D, 24tl iStockphoto.com/inides, 26tl iStockphoto.com/carbouval